I0752765

Dedicated to:

All who wish to open their heart
and mind, to learn, to grow,
to consider things differently

Other Publications by this Author:

The Voyage: Finding the Beautiful Gems of My Being
The Voyage: All Age Coloring Book
Volume 1- Positive Quotes with Author Holly
30 day Gratitude/JOY Pocket Journal
90 day Gratitude/JOY Pocket Journal
90 day Daily Self-Care Accountability Logbook
90 day Daily Self-Care Accountability Log/ Reflect Journal
30 day Daily Self-Care Accountability Logbook
Volume 3- Positive Quotes with Author Holly
30 day Daily Self-Care Accountability Log/ Reflect Journal

Joyful Navigations

Positive Quotes with Author Holly

Volume 2

Holly Ruttenbur Dickinson

Positive Quotes with Author Holly, Volume 2
by Holly Ruttenbur Dickinson.

Book of Quotes.

Joyful Navigations/Trade Name
Joyful Navigations™
Published by Shifting Open LLC.

Self-Help, Personal Growth, Happiness, Success, Motivational, Inspirational, Soul

Book Design, Graphics, Quote Design by Holly Dickinson

Printed in the United States of America

ISBN: 978-1-7355347-3-2

Table of Contents

May you have a MAGNIFICENT day. Take nothing for granted my friends.

©Holly Ruttenbur Dickinson

joyfulnavigations.com

Love yourself enough to look back on your life with TENDERNESS, KINDNESS, FORGIVENESS, and LOVE. You always did the best you knew at the time or were in state of growth and learning and expanding of yourself.

©Holly Ruttenbur Dickinson

AUTHOR HOLLY

joyfulnavigations.com

When you're ready to manifest it, you spend the time focusing on it and taking the actions necessary to bring it to fruition.

©Holly Ruttenbur Dickinson

AUTHOR HOLLY

joyfulnavigations.com

Focus on what brings you JOY! Build those things into your day.

©Holly Ruttenbur Dickinson

AUTHOR HOLLY

joyfulnavigations.com

I'm, "in better service" for you, when I'm taking good care of me.

©Holly Ruttenbur Dickinson

joyfulnavigations.com

Sometimes, you have to have boundaries with yourself.

©Holly Ruttenbur Dickinson

joyfulnavigations.com

Forgiveness...
It means you don't
stay stuck on that one
chapter and miss finding
out how incredible the rest
of the story unfolds.

joyfulnavigations.com

Such wisdom has
been gained from both
the ups and the downs through
life. I appreciate both, now,
more than I ever have.

joyfulnavigations.com

Commit to yourself by committing to a daily step toward your soul's dreams. Even small steps daily will get you there... Vision. Dedication. Consistency.

©Holly Ruttenbur Dickinson

joyfulnavigations.com

I awaken incredible JOY within, incredible peace within, when I am enjoying the stillness in the moment, the beauty in the moment.

©Holly Ruttenbur Dickinson

joyfulnavigations.com

You can only bring change with honesty.

©Holly Ruttenbur Dickinson

joyfulnavigations.com

When I was going through my greatest pain, I know I hurt some people's hearts. I am so sorry.

©Holly Ruttenbur Dickinson

joyfulnavigations.com

When someone says,
"You, Do You!"

To me that is one of the most loving statements someone can say. To me it says, "I'm not here to control you, just love you. Be who you are!"

©Holly Ruttenbur Dickinson

joyfulnavigations.com

The reality is, not everything we want is right for our path or not the right timing.

©Holly Ruttenbur Dickinson

joyfulnavigations.com

Let's choose KINDNESS and respect of one another. We are all in this together.

©Holly Ruttenbur Dickinson

joyfulnavigation.com

I was tired of feeling awful!!
I decided I was worthy of feeling GREAT!!

©Holly Ruttenbur Dickinson

joyfulnavigation.com

Hope...
has saved me
'many a times'.

©Holly Ruttenbur Dickinson

joyfulnavigations.com

Sometimes
taking a pause
to realign is critical
and then readjust
and redirect.

©Holly Ruttenbur Dickinson

joyfulnavigations.com

Our thoughts, habits, routines, and feelings each day, make up our realities.

©Holly Ruttenbur Dickinson

joyfulnavigations.com

A true act of kindness is not meant to be a "favor" to be collected upon later. A true act of kindness comes from the HEART and SEEKS NOTHING in return.

©Holly Ruttenbur Dickinson

joyfulnavigations.come

I used to think
I had to do it all
and be it all. So
glad I was wrong
and know it now.

joyfulnavigations.com

There is a
purpose in all things
whether we understand
those purposes
or not.

joyfulnavigations.com

It's about having the courage to step into our purpose, afraid or not. To just go for it. I knew there were things holding me back and so I took the scary and painful journey to remove those blocks. And here we are.

©Holly Ruttenbur Dickinson

joyfulnavigations.com

Seeing your own growth, fills your soul with delight. Brightens that JOY.

©Holly Ruttenbur Dickinson

joyfulnavigations.com

ALL perspectives need tuning. Because as we learn from our experiences, WE change.

©Holly Ruttenbur Dickinson

joyfulnavigations.com

If you give up, you'll prove them right. Do you really want to do that? Or, do you want them to see, you could achieve your dreams no matter what they believed? Believe so strongly in your dreams that nothing will stop you. Not even their words.

©Holly Ruttenbur Dickinson

joyfulnavigations.com

Setbacks bring an opportunity to look at the situation from a wiped clean new perspective. A chance to step back, breathe, settle on a resolve to try something new, instead of fighting what isn't working.

AUTHOR HOLLY

©Holly Ruttenbur Dickinson

joyfulnavigations.com

When GRATITUDE is my daily practice, everything has a brighter side to it.

©Holly Ruttenbur Dickinson

joyfulnavigations.com

Sometimes,
it will be necessary
to stand alone. Have
the courage.

AUTHOR HOLLY

©Holly Ruttenbur Dickinson

joyfulnavigations.com

And then one day...
YOU understand how to
NOT care what the world wants
from you any longer and YOU start
BEING who YOUR SOUL
KNOWS YOU ARE!

©Holly Ruttenbur Dickinson

joyfulnavigations.com

It takes true strength, courage, and desire to break the patterns of the old you, so you can step into the true potential of who you truly are at your core... the one your soul knows.

©Holly Ruttenbur Dickinson

AUTHOR HOLLY

joyfulnavigations.com

We don't choose what people do. We can only choose FOR OURSELVES... what we do.

AUTHOR HOLLY

©Holly Ruttenbur Dickinson

joyfulnavigations.com

When we force, things can turn out even worse. We do the work necessary and then... the right doors will open.

©Holly Ruttenbur Dickinson

joyfulnavigations.com

What you do with the harsh challenges in life, is what shapes you!! What will you CHOOSE to do with yours?

©Holly Ruttenbur Dickinson

joyfulnavigations.com

As I heal,
I'm feeling the
hard parts within me,
start to soften. What
a beautiful feeling.

©Holly Ruttenbur Dickinson

joyfulnavigations.com

Sometimes integrity calls YOU
to stand up for what is right and true
FOR YOU. Maybe nobody stands with
you and maybe some do. If integrity
calls, you must stand. Not ego, integrity.
To deny standing in your integrity
is to betray even YOUR VERY SOUL.

©Holly Ruttenbur Dickinson

joyfulnavigations.com

Daily FOCUS on your
JOY creates a healthy habit.
Repetition initiates the brain
to create a new way
of BEING.

AUTHOR HOLLY

©Holly Ruttenbur Dickinson

joyfulnavigations.com

It was through
completely losing myself,
that I found myself, my rebirth,
in alignment with my soul.

©Holly Ruttenbur Dickinson

joyfulnavigations.com

Deep breath in
and exhaling it all.

What a journey...
to get to this inner PEACE ,
inner JOY, and inner
KNOWING.

joyfulnavigations.com

When a blessing
comes YOUR way,
don't question it. Embrace it,
be JOYFUL about it, and say
thank you, thank you,
thank you!

AUTHOR HOLLY

joyfulnavigations.com

It feels so much better
having an open heart.
A closed heart hurts.

joyfulnavigations.com

GRATEFUL
for laughter with
good friends and family.
It's such a great feeling to
just laugh and
BE JOYFUL.

AUTHOR HOLLY

joyfulnavigations.com

Sometimes when you look back at things, just looking at the facts, you see a whole different reality than when you were in it. Time, space, healing, and growth, can allow for an adjusted perspective that take out the feelings and show just the facts of what was. What an enlightened perspective it can bring.

AUTHOR HOLLY

joyfulnavigations.com

Many, do not break
away from the crowd, to
follow the calling of their soul.
Courageous, are the
ones that do.

©Holly Ruttenbur Dickinson

joyfulnavigations.com

If your future self could
send a message of 3 words
to your past and current self
over and over through the
years, what would those
3 words be?

©Holly Ruttenbur Dickinson

joyfulnavigations.com

It took sooooo
much courage to face
and heal the deep wounds
that compelled certain behaviors.
In doing so, has positively
shifted my life.

AUTHOR HOLLY

joyfulnavigations.com

Choose to make
GRATITUDE and JOY
daily habits. Choose to
make them YOUR way of
being. It is possible. It
takes practice.

AUTHOR HOLLY

joyfulnavigations.com

It takes awareness
to not take someone's
"bad day" personal.

©Holly Ruttenbur Dickinson

joyfulnavigations.com

Some people think
that relationships are games.
That mentality, will NOT build a
precious, respectful, honorable,
lasting relationship.

©Holly Ruttenbur Dickinson

joyfulnavigations.com

Each time
you walk through the
fear, FACE ON, it helps you
to become stronger, braver,
and more courageous
for the next time.

AUTHOR HOLLY

©Holy Ruttenbur Dickinson

joyfulnavigations.com

We cannot help heal
the world until we can
heal ourselves FIRST!

©Holly Ruttenbur Dickinson

joyfulnavigations.org

People don't always show up the way we are hoping they will. Practice being bendable so it doesn't break you!

AUTHOR HOLLY

©Holly Ruttenbur Dickinson

joyfulnavigations.com

Sometimes people come into our lives and wake up a part of us that has been lying dormant. It sets us on a different path. And it changes us forever.

AUTHOR HOLLY

©Holly Ruttenbur Dickinson

joyfulnavigations.com

Each person needs
to find their OWN way
to PEACE. It's an individual
journey that affects
the whole.

©Holy Ruttenbur Dickinson

joyfulnavigations.com

May you dedicate
yourself to a more JOYful
life through GRATITUDE.

©Holly Ruttenbur Dickinson

joyfulnavigations.org

Helping
others can bring
you incredible
JOY.

AUTHOR HOLLY

joyfulnavigations.com

A daily act
of KINDNESS does
something for your
well being.

AUTHOR HOLLY

joyfulnavigations.com

Excuses keep people from achieving their dreams and goals.

AUTHOR HOLLY

©Holly Ruttenbur Dickinson

joyfulnavigations.com

Pain, is part of the journey. Not all of the journey, but part. We must know it, to respect its true value.

AUTHOR HOLLY

©Holly Ruttenbur Dickinson

joyfulnavigations.com

You are a beautiful SHINING LIGHT. I hope you don't hide it any longer.

©Holly Ruttenbur Dickinson

joyfulnavigations.com

You are stronger than you give yourself credit for. We were made for survival. You've got this!!

©Holly Ruttenbur Dickinson

joyfulnavigations.com

May YOU
find YOUR peace
and calmness
WITHIN you.

AUTHOR HOLLY

©Holly Ruttenbur Dickinson

joyfulnavigations.com

Our unhealed
wounds hold us back.
Heal your wounds to
awaken YOUR
inner JOY.

AUTHOR HOLLY

©Holly Ruttenbur Dickinson

joyfulnavigations.com

Positive Quotes with Author Holly Volume 1 and Volume 2
Full color quotes

30 day and 90 day Gratitude/JOY Pocket Journal
Black and white inside

30 and 90 day Daily Self-Care Accountability Logbook and Logbook with Reflection Journal
Black and white inside

The Voyage
Finding the Beautiful Gems of My Being
Fully Illustrated with 20 watercolor paintings

The Voyage.
Coloring Book
For All Ages
Black and white coloring pages of all the illustrations of the original book.

A Message from the Author

It's exciting that my 2nd little pocketbook of quotes is already out. I was so pumped from doing Volume 1 that I just kept going. Since I'm on a roll, I've already started Volume 3. As in each volume that I bring forth, my wish for you is the same… I hope that something in my writings has inspired you and/or brought some new awareness to your thinking. Maybe it has given you some new perspectives to consider, prompted growth or prompted changed behavior. Hopefully something here has helped you smile, brought you joy, or set you on a journey to become a better you.
~Author Holly, Your Joyful Guide

Visit me on the Facebook Page:
Positive Quotes with Author Holly and
Choose Joyful with Joyful Navigations™
Website: https://joyfulnavigations.com

About the Author

Author Holly R. Dickinson is a Lightworker and a Mass Influencer of 7 million plus followers on her Facebook Page. She is a Mother of 4, now adults. She is in a loving marriage to her husband of 27 years. Early life brought many traumas and challenges to her. She shares her wisdom, perspectives, and courage in her writings. God, love, kindness, gratitude, family, awareness, courage, action, trust, compassion, forgiveness, self-care, positivity, and choosing joy are key for her.

www.ingramcontent.com/pod-product-compliance
Lightning Source LLC
LaVergne TN
LVHW052357100826
845147LV00013B/866

* 9 7 8 1 7 3 5 5 3 4 7 3 2 *